Mathematical Treasure-Hunts

Enjoyable activities to enhance the curriculum

Vivien Lucas

Contents

Tarquin Publications

301 287

Introduction

Welcome to this book about mathematical treasure-hunts. It is written mainly for teachers but the ideas can easily be adapted for use as party games for almost any age group. All of the quiz questions given as examples are based on mathematical ideas but of course the principles of organisation could be used for other subjects too. A treasure-hunt is a 'fun idea' but there is no reason at all why the actual questions cannot contain 'meat' and be quite demanding. Obviously the level can be easily adjusted and adapted to a specific class or group.

First thoughts about organising a treasure-hunt might well suggest writing a series of questions on cards and then pinning them around the classroom or a larger area. While this would undoubtedly work, it is essentially not very different from an ordinary written test. The only mystery is to find where the questions are pinned up!

The method suggested and recommended in this book is to set the questions into a specific order and to show the answer to the previous question prominently at the head of each card.

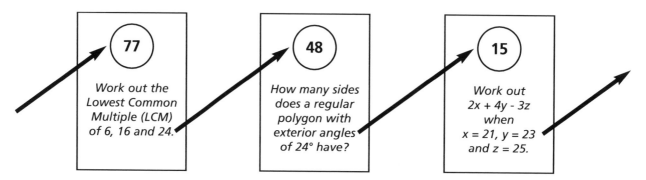

This technique organises the complete treasure-hunt into a 'cyclic' loop.

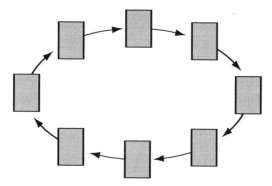

The logical order of the questions can be represented like this.

However, since the cards are in fact arranged at random around the room or locality, the actual route followed by the contestants is more like this.

How many questions are required?

The difficulty and level of the problems has an obvious influence on the total time taken as does the extent of the area over which the clues are spread. If you have not tried such an activity before with one of your classes, then it is a good idea to try a short demonstration with say 6-8 clues and see how it goes and how long it lasts. As the number of clues increases so does the time the treasure-hunt takes and the increase is rather greater than the strict proportion, probably because it takes longer to physically search for a card with the right answer on it.

1. A treasure-hunt with 6 clues lasts about 10 minutes and is ideal for an open day when the idea is to provide 'tasters' for all kinds of activities.
2. A treasure-hunt with 10 to 12 clues lasts between 20 minutes and half an hour.
3. A treasure-hunt with 12 to 24 clues lasts between three-quarters of an hour and an hour.
4. It is probably inadvisable to try a treasure-hunt with more than 24 clues unless you have a group who are really enthusiastic. For most groups interest will begin to wane if it goes on too long.

How to organise a cyclic treasure-hunt

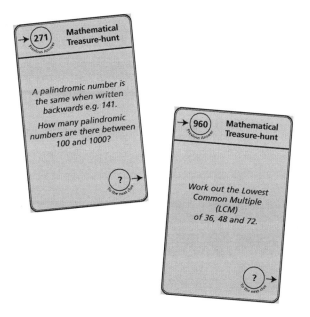

271 Mathematical Treasure-hunt
Previous Answer

A palindromic number is the same when written backwards e.g. 141.

How many palindromic numbers are there between 100 and 1000?

? To the next clue

960 Mathematical Treasure-hunt
Previous Answer

Work out the Lowest Common Multiple (LCM) of 36, 48 and 72.

? To the next clue

It is best to start with one of the photocopiable treasure-hunts provided in this book. They are tried and tested and it will soon become apparent if the questions are too easy or too hard for a particular group. Copy the cards and trim them to remove the page headers. For a first trial it is not necessary to laminate them. Then arrange the cards around the classroom, hall or corridors or indeed outside if the weather is suitable. If you place them in the order of the reference numbers you can be certain that the logical order of answering them is very different and that no consecutive answers are next to each other.

Duplicate sufficient blank answer sheets so that there is one for each team and a few to spare. Write a different number from the answers in the top left corner of each and hand one to each team. This ensures that all the teams begin at a different card and so are well spread out. It also has the benefit that all the answer sheets appear at first glance to be different. This makes it surprisingly difficult for one team at a glance to spot a missing answer on the answer sheet of another team. Of course, in reality, the cyclic order is the same for all contestants but none the less they do appear different because of their different starting points. A decision needs to be made about whether or not calculators are permitted.

Explain the rules of the treasure-hunt before saying 'go' to start everyone off. Each team has to start by finding the 'answer' at the head of a card. Of course it is the answer to an as yet unknown question.

The contestants solve the puzzle or problem and write the answer into the next empty circle of the answer sheet. They then look for that answer at the head of another card. So it continues until the answer to one of the questions is the number they were first given. The treasure-hunt is then complete and it can either be handed in or they can do some 'bonus questions' as suggested on page 35.

How many people in a team?

If there is an even number of contestants then they can all work in pairs and there is no problem. In my experience three or more in a team is too many as it is then only too easy to avoid making a contribution. If there should be an odd number of contestants, there may be one pupil who is quite happy to work alone. Depending on the circumstances, however, it may be preferable for the teacher to decide the composition of the teams. If the pairing is to be left to personal choice and one person does need to work alone, then it is definitely preferable for that person to be selected initially and openly by the teacher by drawing a card or a ticket. Then the others must then pair off evenly to complete the teams and no-one is left over at the end.

The rules for the contestants

1. Each team needs an answer sheet, pen or pencil, spare paper for working out and a calculator if allowed. Clip boards are also useful but not essential.
2. The members of a team must stay together to answer the questions.
3. The team must start at the allocated starting number and work round in order.
4. No-one must move the clues or write on them.
5. If help is needed, teachers will only answer 'yes' or 'no'.
   You will need to phrase your questions carefully.
6. Don't let other teams see your answer sheet.
7. You finish when you get back to where you started.
8. Hand in your answer sheet as soon as you have finished so that the time can be recorded and the sequence of answers can be checked.

Devising a treasure-hunt of your own

The first stage is to make up the required number of questions and to put each one on to a separate A5 sheet of paper. It is at this stage it must be decided whether or not calculators should be permitted. As a general rule it is probably better that they are not. However, as a special event it would not be at all difficult to construct a treasure-hunt where all the questions definitely required the use of one.

Initially it is best to write the answer to the problem at the foot of the sheet, perhaps in an ink of a different colour. This is the occasion for checking that no two questions have the same answer and then modifying one of them if they do. This is vital.

Then arrange the puzzles into an order in which they will be answered. This offers a chance to separate any problems which might be thought to cover similar ideas. Once the sequence is determined, write the answer to the previous question at the head of each paper. Finally, give each a reference number making sure that the order of the reference numbers does not correspond to the order of the answers. A random mixture is best.

The actual design will no doubt be personal to the designer but there are three features which should be included. Cards of A5 size are probably large enough for most situations.

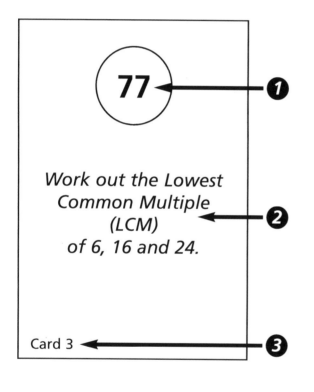

1. The answer to the previous question should be prominently displayed at the head of each card. Since it is the means by which contestants navigate themselves around the treasure-hunt, it must be large and bold enough.

2. The puzzle itself should not be too 'wordy', but should be interesting and challenging at the level intended.

All questions should be phrased to produce an integer answer. Where units are involved, care should be taken to phrase the question so that it produces an answer which is a number. For instance: 'How many metres is it....?' rather than 'How far is it...?'

3. There should be a reference number. This is purely for the convenience of the organiser. It makes it easier to check that all the cards are there or to identify which is missing. For obvious reasons it is essential that the reference number order is **not** the same as the logical order of the puzzles!

These days it is probably best if the actual cards can be produced on a computer using a graphics package. The ones provided in this collection were drawn in Adobe Illustrator on a Macintosh. Others might prefer to use Freehand or Corel Draw or other programs with which they are already familiar. Otherwise, it is surprising how much can be achieved with a word processor, a pair of scissors and some glue. All these suggestions ignore those with a fine calligraphic hand and the ability to draw. The point being made here is that the more professionally produced the whole treasure-hunt looks, the more likely it is to be taken seriously.

While presentation is important, of much greater importance is the selection of good and interesting problems and in tuning them to the level and ability of the group or class.

A well constructed treasure-hunt is a resource that can be reused for many years. It is a simple matter to laminate the cards or to place them in sealable transparent pockets to give them the extra strength and longevity which is desirable.

How to create answer sheets

Each team should have an answer sheet with the appropriate number of linked circles on it and this recommended format reinforces the notion that the treasure-hunt is cyclic. For this reason it is important to supply answer sheets with the exact number of spaces for the current treasure-hunt. Contestants can then see easily and naturally how many more cards there are to do.

In addition, if a wrong answer leads to a short circuit and a return to the start too quickly, the team still has the opportunity to find the error and so complete the whole treasure-hunt correctly and within the time allowed.

For 6, 10 or 12 cards, an A5 sheet of paper is probably large enough for recording the answers. However for 24 clues it is best that it is A4.

While answer sheets can be produced from scratch, perhaps by drawing round a small coin, it may be found to be more convenient to use or make one of the masters provided.

This is the suggested method:

For a treasure-hunt of 24 clues, make a photocopy of page 36. and use it as it stands. You need one answer sheet for each team and a few spares.

For treasure-hunts of between 12 and 22 clues, still photocopy page 36 but then cut off the bottom row of circles and make a new master. Simply glue it further up the page. The arrows will still point in the correct directions and with care the join will hardly show.

For the given sets with 6 and 10 clues or your own treasure-hunts of the same sizes, suitable A5 masters are given on page 6. They can be photocopied directly.

The answers to the given sets are printed at reduced size inside the back cover. You may find it more convenient to fill in one of the full-size answer sheets with the answers and to use it for checking.

Special points to consider

One characteristic of this kind of cyclic treasure-hunt is that it becomes very difficult for a team to continue without help if they are unable to solve one of the puzzles. Progress cannot be made without a correct answer to lead to the next card and a teacher with a complete set of answers needs to be on hand. It is good practice to strictly limit the amount of help available and to set up the rule that teachers will only answer questions with a 'yes' or a 'no'. Questions like 'Is 27 the answer to card 9?' Answer 'No'. A few pertinent questions will soon get the team back on course. If the clues are spread through several rooms, it is a good idea to have a teacher with the answers in each of them.

Another problem which can arise is when a wrong answer leads to a later card in the sequence, so short-circuiting the whole treasure-hunt. Most groups will soon realise and get back on track but help may be needed.

Answer Sheet

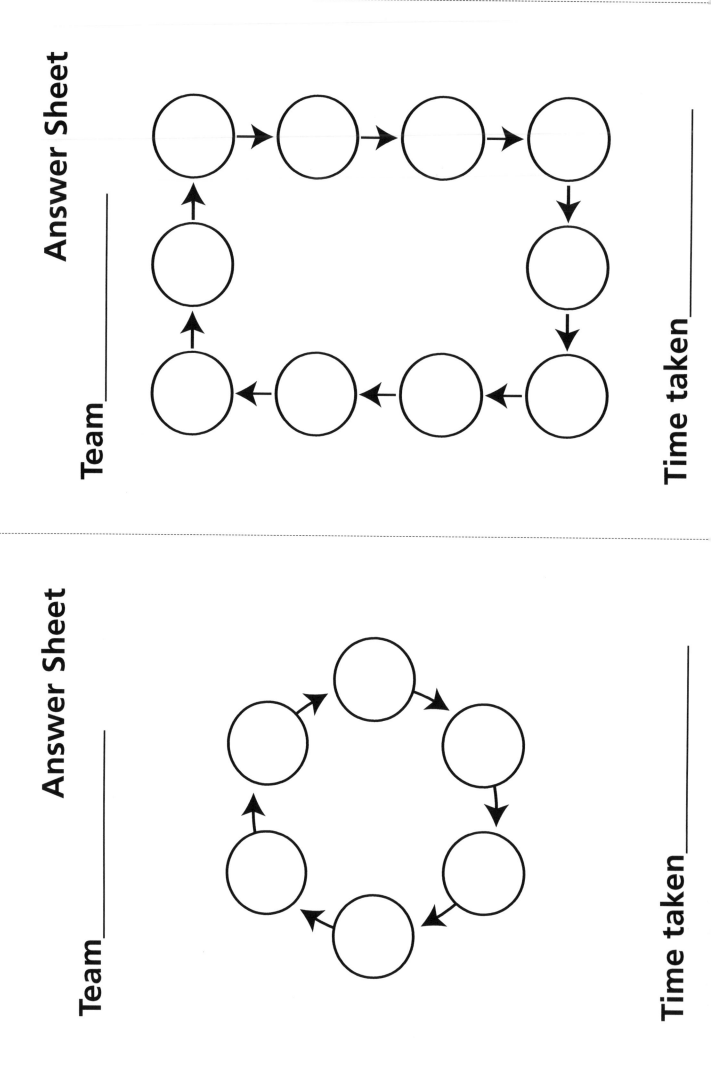

Team _____

Time taken _____

Answer Sheet

Team _____

Time taken _____

Mathematical Treasure-hunt

Previous Answer **11**

Think of a number.

Double it.

Add 6.

Halve it.

Take away your first number.

What is left?

Hint:
Check with a different number

? To the next clue

Set A: Card 2 of 6

Mathematical Treasure-hunt

Previous Answer **9**

Circle Men Maths

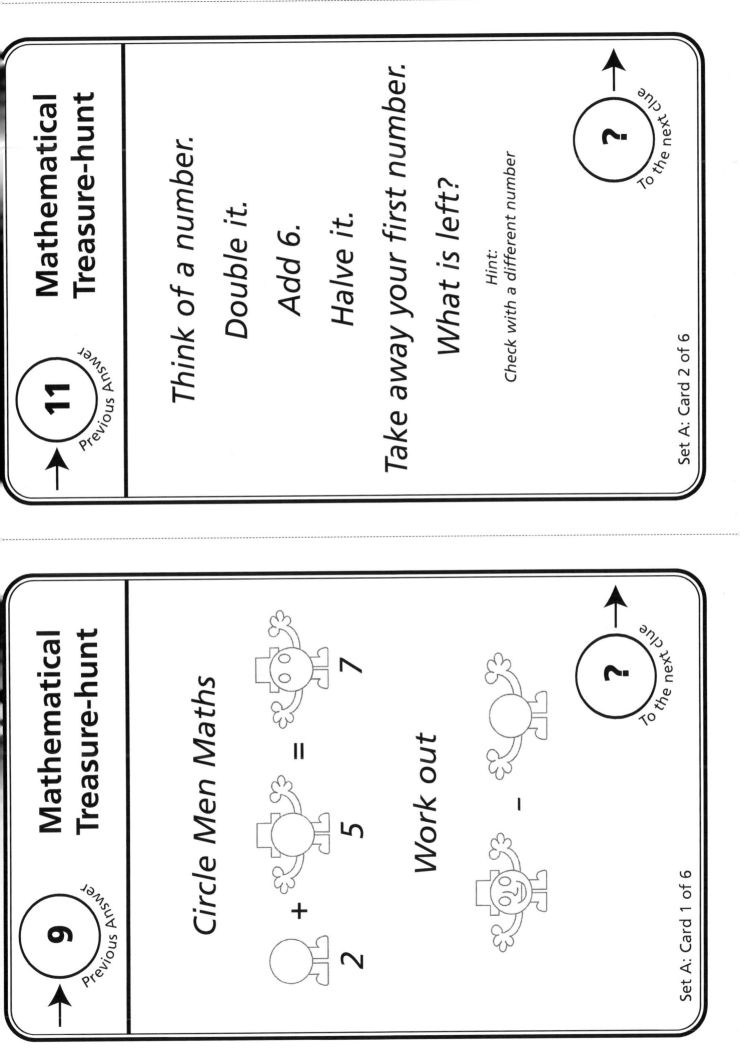

2 + 5 = 7

Work out

? To the next clue

Set A: Card 1 of 6

Mathematical Treasure-hunt

3

Previous Answer

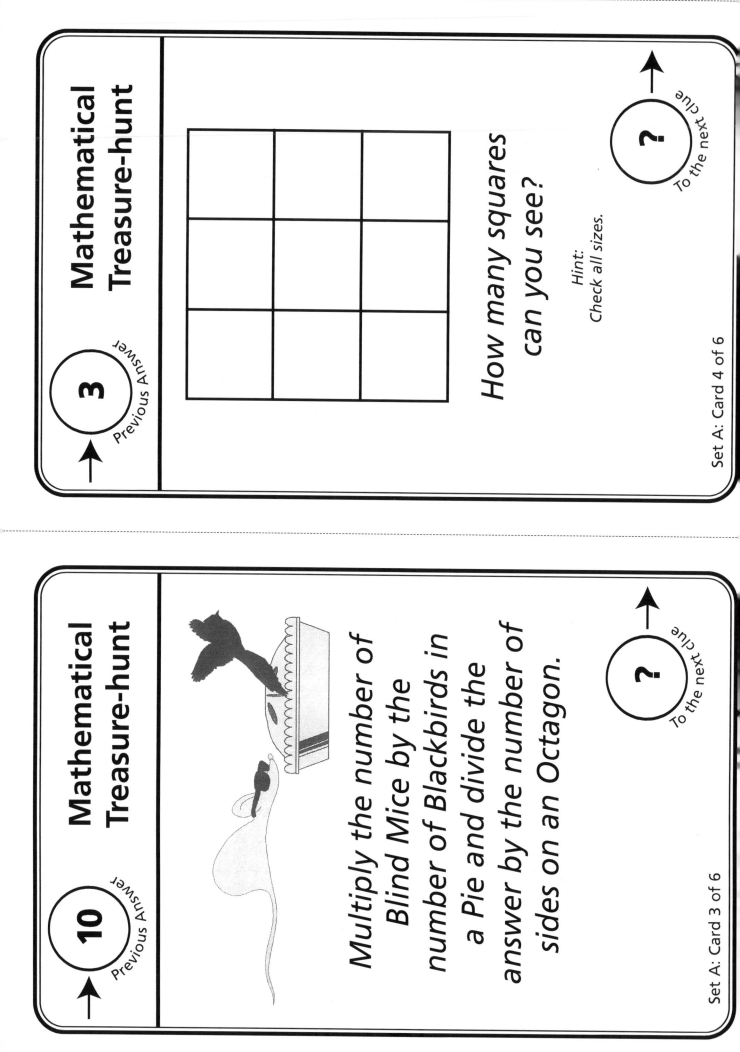

How many squares can you see?

Hint:
Check all sizes.

?

To the next clue

Set A: Card 4 of 6

Mathematical Treasure-hunt

10

Previous Answer

Multiply the number of Blind Mice by the number of Blackbirds in a Pie and divide the answer by the number of sides on an Octagon.

?

To the next clue

Set A: Card 3 of 6

Mathematical Treasure-hunt

14 Previous Answer

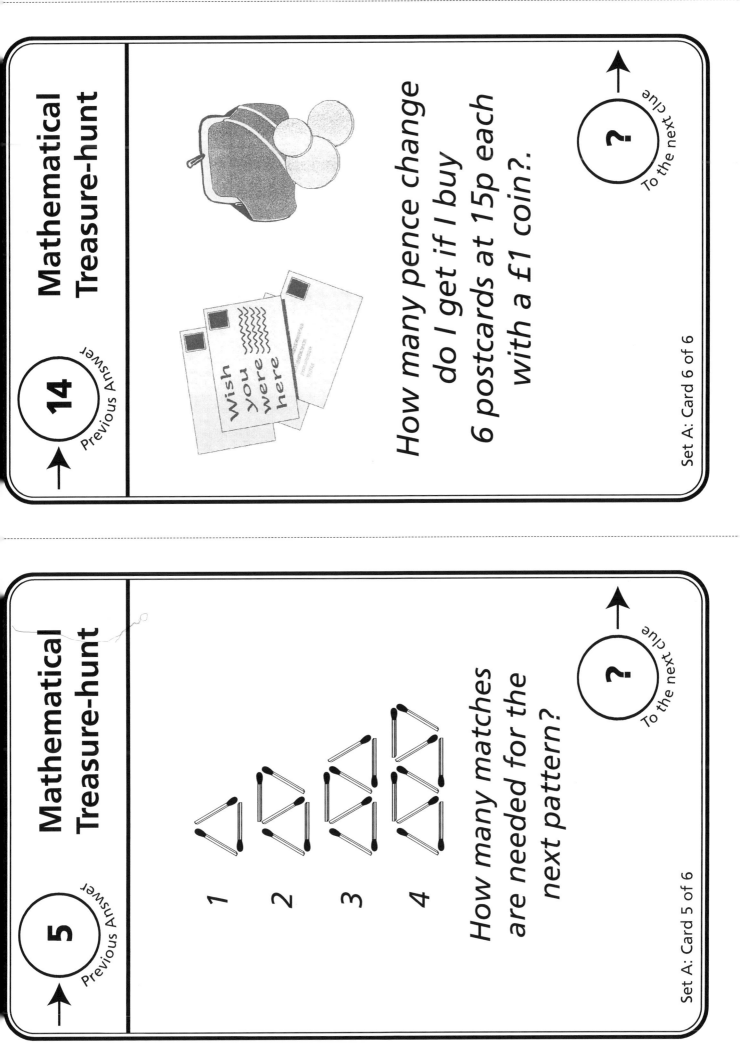

How many pence change do I get if I buy 6 postcards at 15p each with a £1 coin?.

? To the next clue

Mathematical Treasure-hunt

5 Previous Answer

1
2
3
4

How many matches are needed for the next pattern?

? To the next clue

Mathematical Treasure-hunt

12 Previous Answer

A factor
is a number
that will divide exactly
into another number
e.g. 5 is a factor of 100.

How many factors has the
number 144?

Hint:
Don't forget 1 and 144!

? To the next clue

Set B: Card 2 of 10

Mathematical Treasure-hunt

55 Previous Answer

Think of a number
Add 3
Multiply by 4
Take away 2
Divide by 2
Add 21
Divide by 2.

Take away the number you
started with and what is left?

Hint:
Check it again with a different starting number.

? To the next clue

Set B: Card 1 of 10

Mathematical Treasure-hunt

15
Previous Answer

Look at these arrangements of matchsticks.

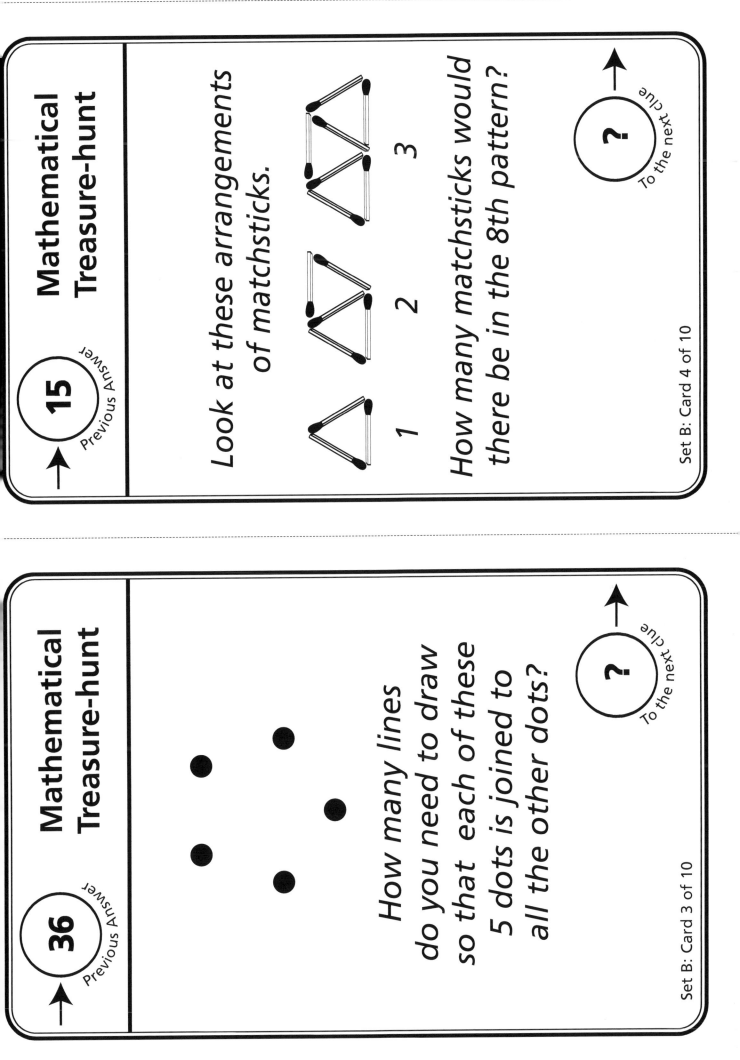

1   2   3

How many matchsticks would there be in the 8th pattern?

?
To the next clue

Set B: Card 4 of 10

Mathematical Treasure-hunt

36
Previous Answer

How many lines do you need to draw so that each of these 5 dots is joined to all the other dots?

?
To the next clue

Set B: Card 3 of 10

Mathematical Treasure-hunt

37 Previous Answer

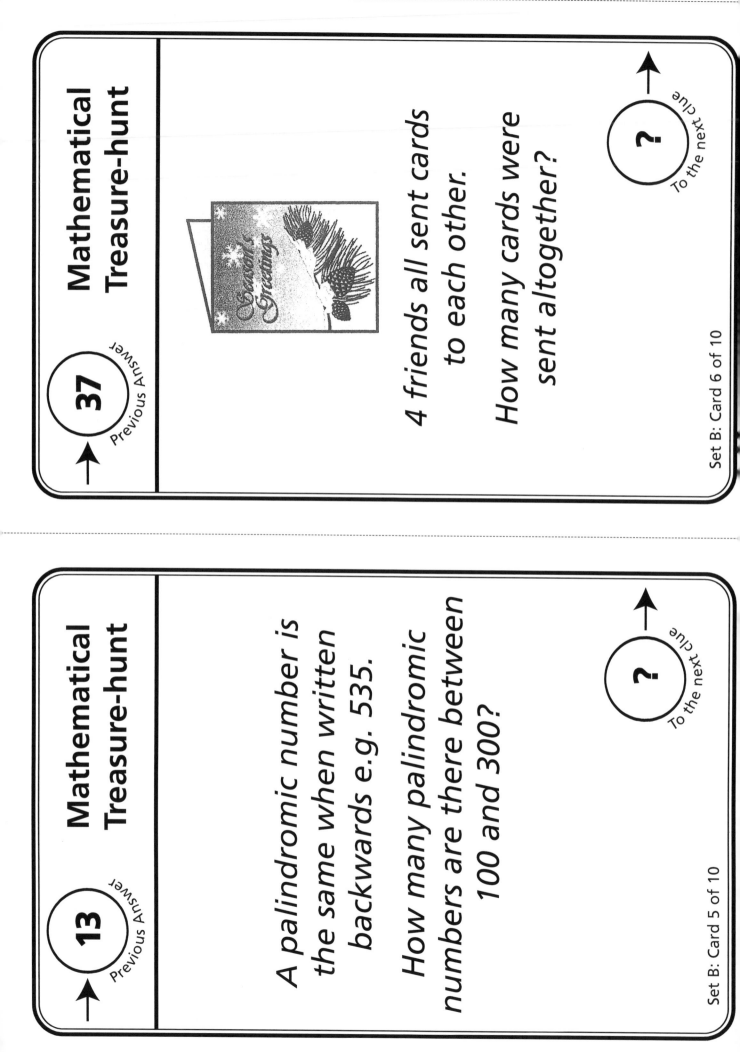

4 friends all sent cards to each other.

How many cards were sent altogether?

? To the next clue

Set B: Card 6 of 10

Mathematical Treasure-hunt

13 Previous Answer

A palindromic number is the same when written backwards e.g. 535.

How many palindromic numbers are there between 100 and 300?

? To the next clue

Set B: Card 5 of 10

Card 8

Mathematical Treasure-hunt

Previous Answer **20**

? + ? = 11

or

? + ? = 13

How many
2 digit numbers
are there where
the sum of the 2 digits
totals 11 or 13?

?

To the next clue

Set B: Card 8 of 10

Card 7

Mathematical Treasure-hunt

Previous Answer **17**

Square Numbers

$1 \times 1 = 1$

$2 \times 2 = 4$

$3 \times 3 = 9$

$4 \times 4 = 16$

Triangular Numbers

1

$1 + 2 = 3$

$1 + 2 + 3 = 6$

$1 + 2 + 3 + 4 = 10$

Find the next number after 1,
that is both a square number
and also a triangular number.

?

To the next clue

Set B: Card 7 of 10

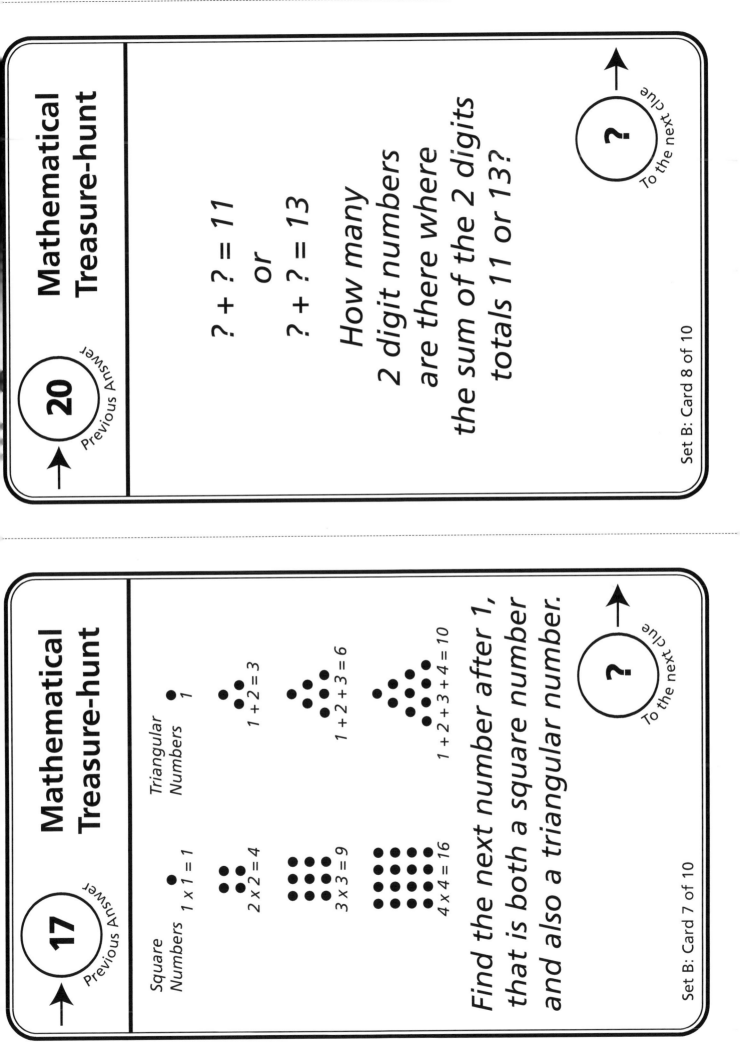

Mathematical Treasure-hunt

14
Previous Answer

A prime number can only be divided by itself and one. (One is not a prime number)

The first prime numbers are: 2, 3, 5, 7, 11 etc.

Work out the twelfth prime number.

?
To the next clue

Set B: Card 10 of 10

Mathematical Treasure-hunt

10
Previous Answer

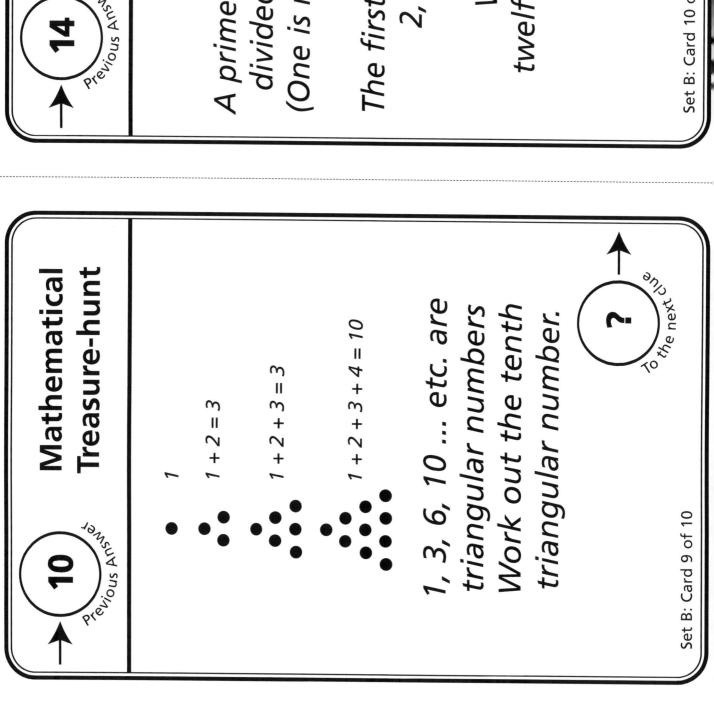

1

1 + 2 = 3

1 + 2 + 3 = 3

1 + 2 + 3 + 4 = 10

1, 3, 6, 10 ... etc. are triangular numbers
Work out the tenth triangular number.

?
To the next clue

Set B: Card 9 of 10

Mathematical Treasure-hunt

Previous Answer: 20

Sir Cumference
The jovial mathematics teacher

Sir asks 'To the nearest centimetre, how much ribbon is needed to go exactly round a cake of radius 10cm?'.

To the next clue ?

Set C: Card 2 of 12

Mathematical Treasure-hunt

Previous Answer: 144

Al Gebra
He loves solving equations.

Al wants to know the value of $3a^2b^3$ when $a = 3$ and $b = 2$.

To the next clue ?

Set C: Card 1 of 12

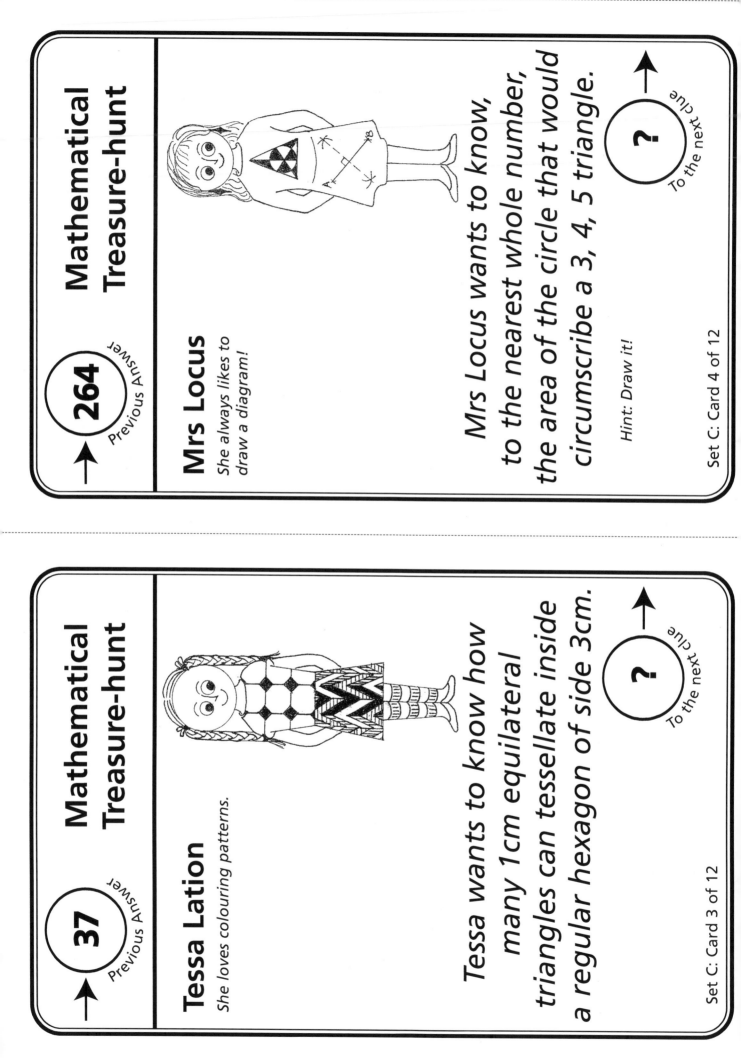

Mathematical Treasure-hunt

Previous Answer

264

Mrs Locus
She always likes to draw a diagram!

Mrs Locus wants to know, to the nearest whole number, the area of the circle that would circumscribe a 3, 4, 5 triangle.

Hint: Draw it!

To the next clue

?

Set C: Card 4 of 12

Mathematical Treasure-hunt

Previous Answer

37

Tessa Lation
She loves colouring patterns.

Tessa wants to know how many 1cm equilateral triangles can tessellate inside a regular hexagon of side 3cm.

To the next clue

?

Set C: Card 3 of 12

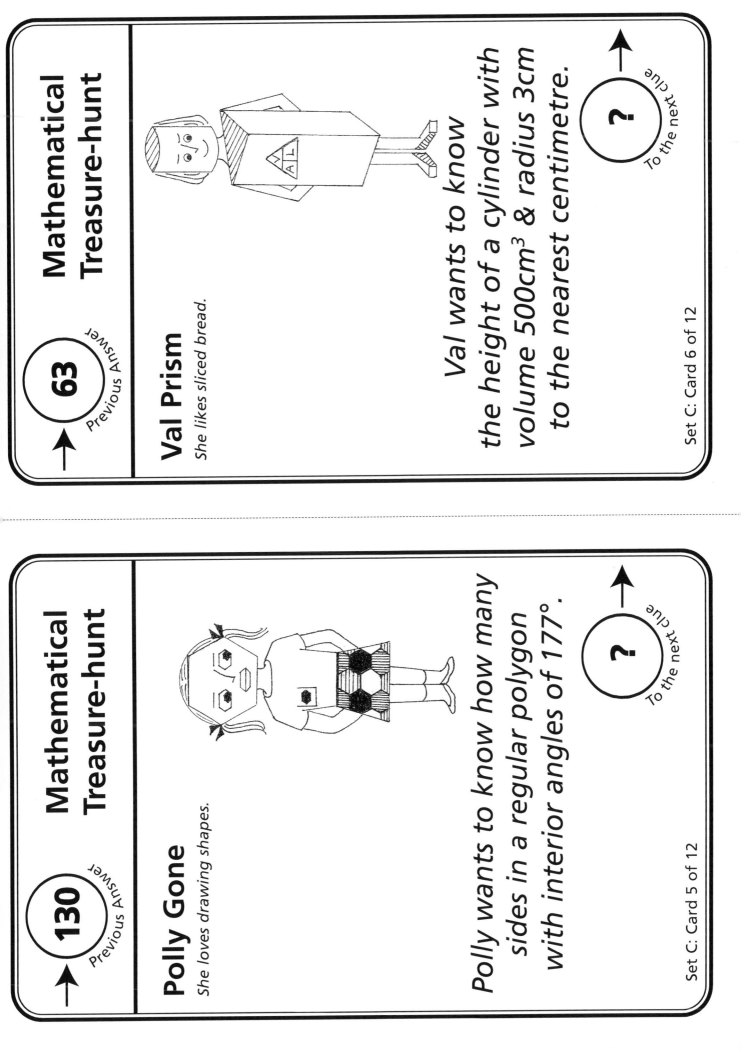

Mathematical Treasure-hunt

63
Previous Answer

Val Prism
She likes sliced bread.

Val wants to know the height of a cylinder with volume 500cm³ & radius 3cm to the nearest centimetre.

?
To the next clue

Set C: Card 6 of 12

Mathematical Treasure-hunt

130
Previous Answer

Polly Gone
She loves drawing shapes.

Polly wants to know how many sides in a regular polygon with interior angles of 177°.

?
To the next clue

Set C: Card 5 of 12

Mathematical Treasure-hunt

54

Previous Answer

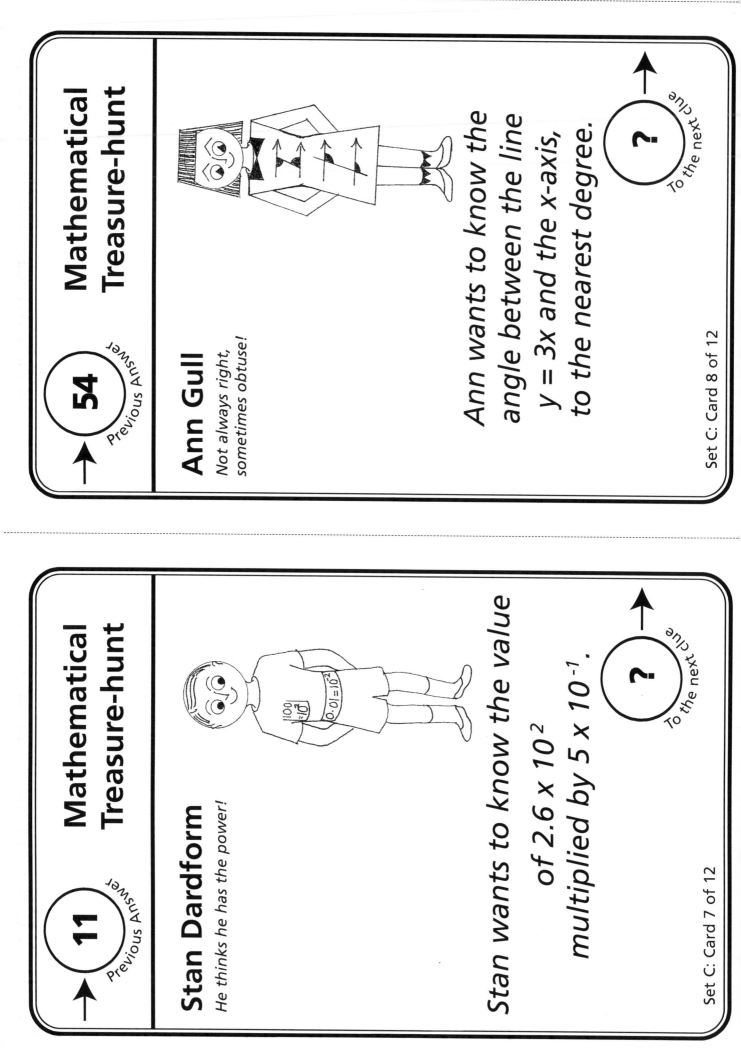

Ann Gull

Not always right, sometimes obtuse!

Ann wants to know the angle between the line y = 3x and the x-axis, to the nearest degree.

?

To the next clue

Set C: Card 8 of 12

Mathematical Treasure-hunt

11

Previous Answer

Stan Dardform

He thinks he has the power!

Stan wants to know the value of 2.6 × 10² multiplied by 5 × 10⁻¹.

?

To the next clue

Set C: Card 7 of 12

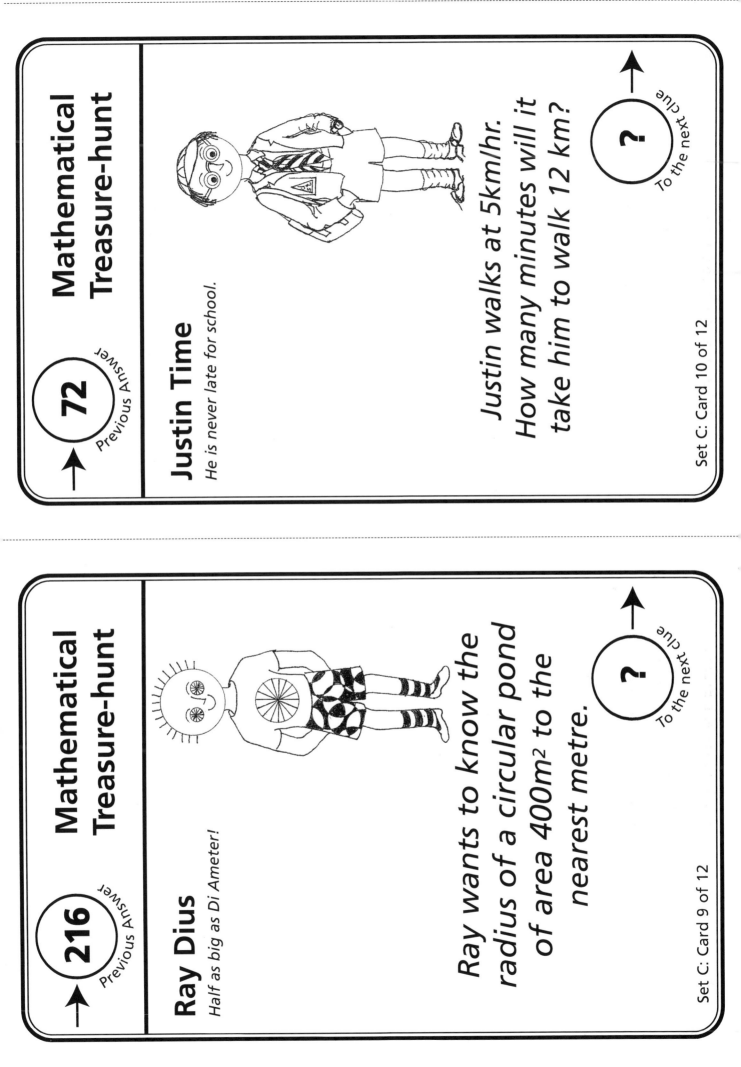

Mathematical Treasure-hunt

72
Previous Answer

Justin Time
He is never late for school.

Justin walks at 5km/hr. How many minutes will it take him to walk 12 km?

?
To the next clue

Set C: Card 10 of 12

Mathematical Treasure-hunt

216
Previous Answer

Ray Dius
Half as big as Di Ameter!

Ray wants to know the radius of a circular pond of area 400m² to the nearest metre.

?
To the next clue

Set C: Card 9 of 12

Mathematical Treasure-hunt

120
Previous Answer

Adam Up
He's a mean guy!

Adam wants to know the sum of the even numbers between 25 & 41.

?
To the next clue

Set C: Card 12 of 12

Mathematical Treasure-hunt

18
Previous Answer

Trigonometry Triplets
From planet OPPADJHYP

The Triplets ask 'What's the size of the smallest angle in a 3,4,5 triangle to the nearest degree?'.

?
To the next clue

Set C: Card 11 of 12

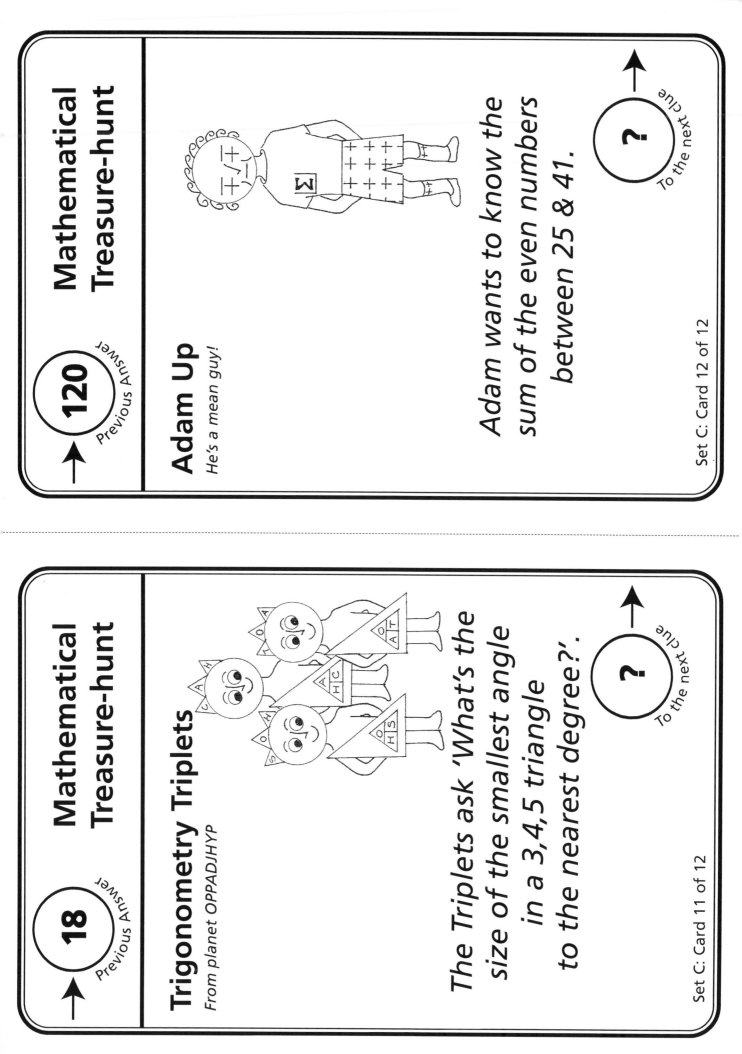

Mathematical Treasure-hunt

(30) Previous Answer

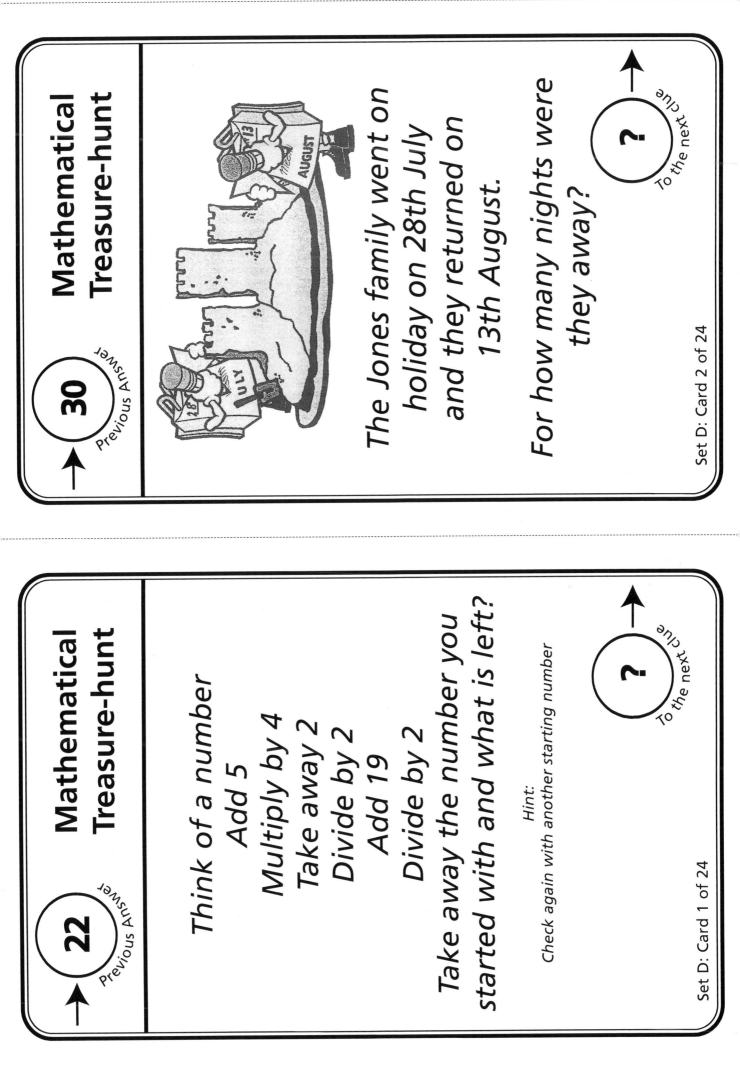

The Jones family went on holiday on 28th July and they returned on 13th August.

For how many nights were they away?

To the next clue

?

Set D: Card 2 of 24

Mathematical Treasure-hunt

(22) Previous Answer

Think of a number
Add 5
Multiply by 4
Take away 2
Divide by 2
Add 19
Divide by 2

Take away the number you started with and what is left?

Hint:
Check again with another starting number

To the next clue

?

Set D: Card 1 of 24

Mathematical Treasure-hunt

24
Previous Answer

Think of a number.
Add 6.
Double it.
Take away 2.
Double it again.
Add 24.
Divide by 4.

Take away the number you started with and what is left?

Hint:
Check again with another starting number

? To the next clue

Set D: Card 4 of 24

Mathematical Treasure-hunt

28
Previous Answer

I thought of a number.
Then I added 2.
Then I multiplied by 4.
Then I divided by 5.
The answer was 20.

What was the number I first thought of?

? To the next clue

Set D: Card 3 of 24

Mathematical Treasure-hunt

16
Previous Answer

If A = 1, B = 2, C = 3, …
… Z = 26, work out
the value of:

M - A + T - H - S

? To the next clue

Mathematical Treasure-hunt

7
Previous Answer

Look at these arrangements
of matchsticks.

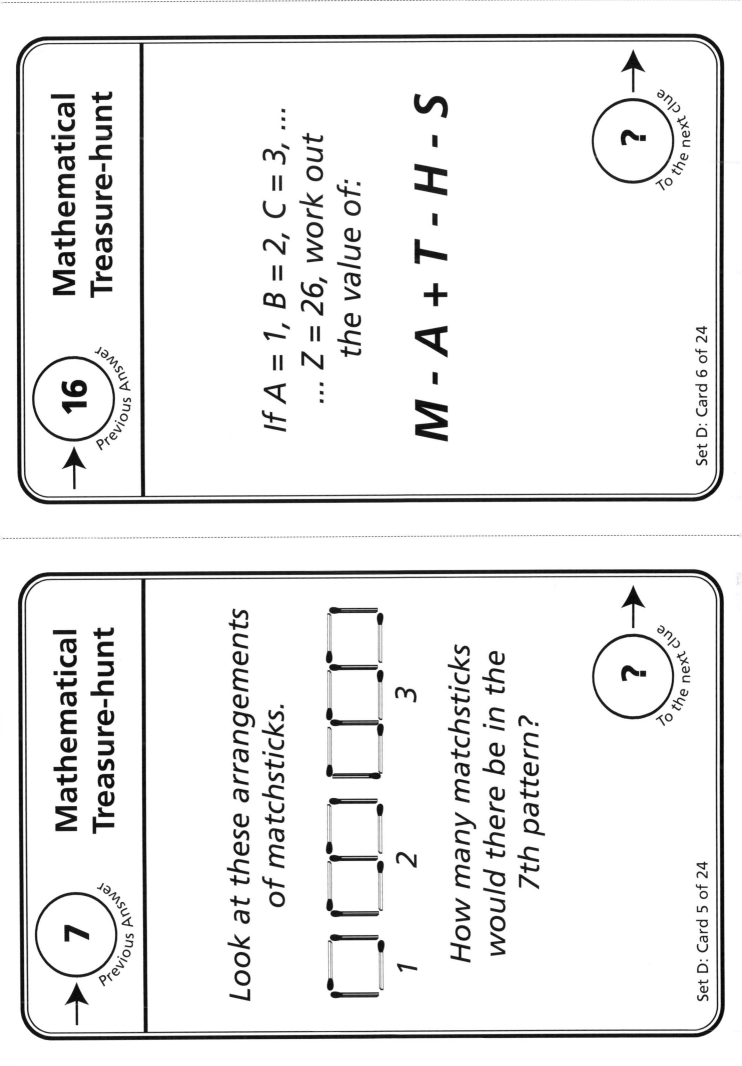

1   2   3

How many matchsticks
would there be in the
7th pattern?

? To the next clue

Card 8

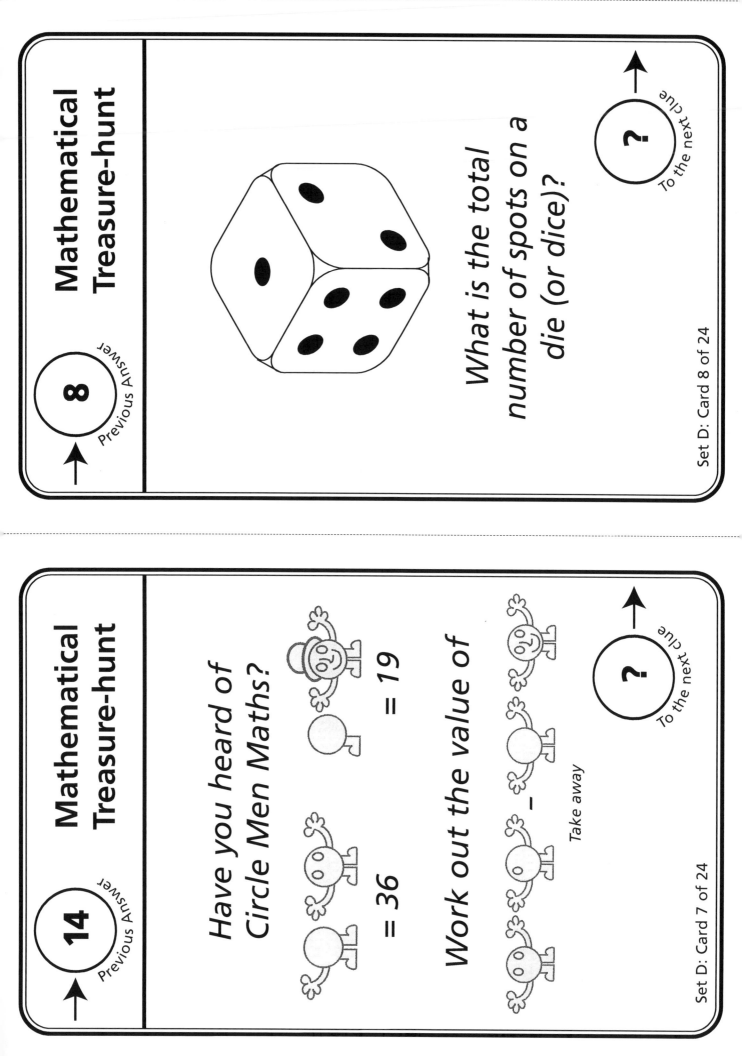

Mathematical Treasure-hunt

8 Previous Answer

What is the total number of spots on a die (or dice)?

? To the next clue

Set D: Card 8 of 24

Card 7

Mathematical Treasure-hunt

14 Previous Answer

Have you heard of Circle Men Maths?

= 36

= 19

Work out the value of

− Take away

? To the next clue

Set D: Card 7 of 24

Mathematical Treasure-hunt

20
Previous Answer

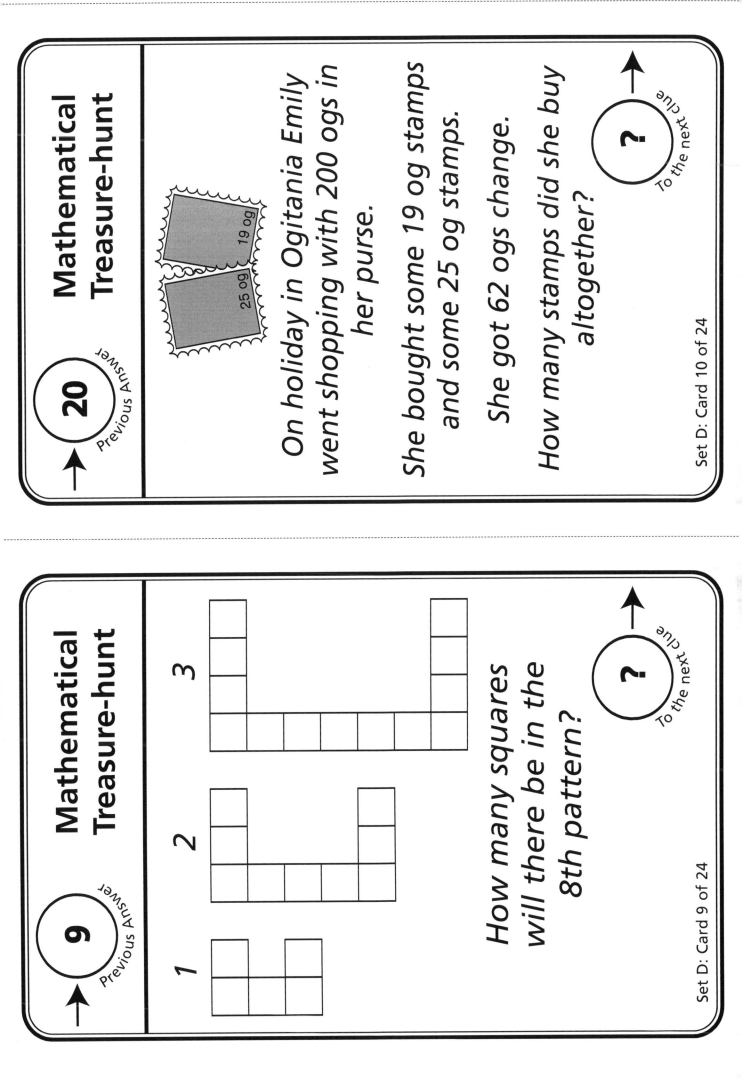

25 og

19 og

On holiday in Ogitania Emily went shopping with 200 ogs in her purse.

She bought some 19 og stamps and some 25 og stamps.

She got 62 ogs change.

How many stamps did she buy altogether?

? To the next clue

Set D: Card 10 of 24

Mathematical Treasure-hunt

9
Previous Answer

1

2

3

How many squares will there be in the 8th pattern?

? To the next clue

Set D: Card 9 of 24

Mathematical Treasure-hunt

5

Previous Answer

In a class of 30 pupils:

Half the class are boys.

One third of the class go to school by bus.

13 boys do <u>not</u> go to school by bus.

How many girls <u>do</u> go to school by bus?

?

To the next clue

Set D: Card 12 of 24

Mathematical Treasure-hunt

10

Previous Answer

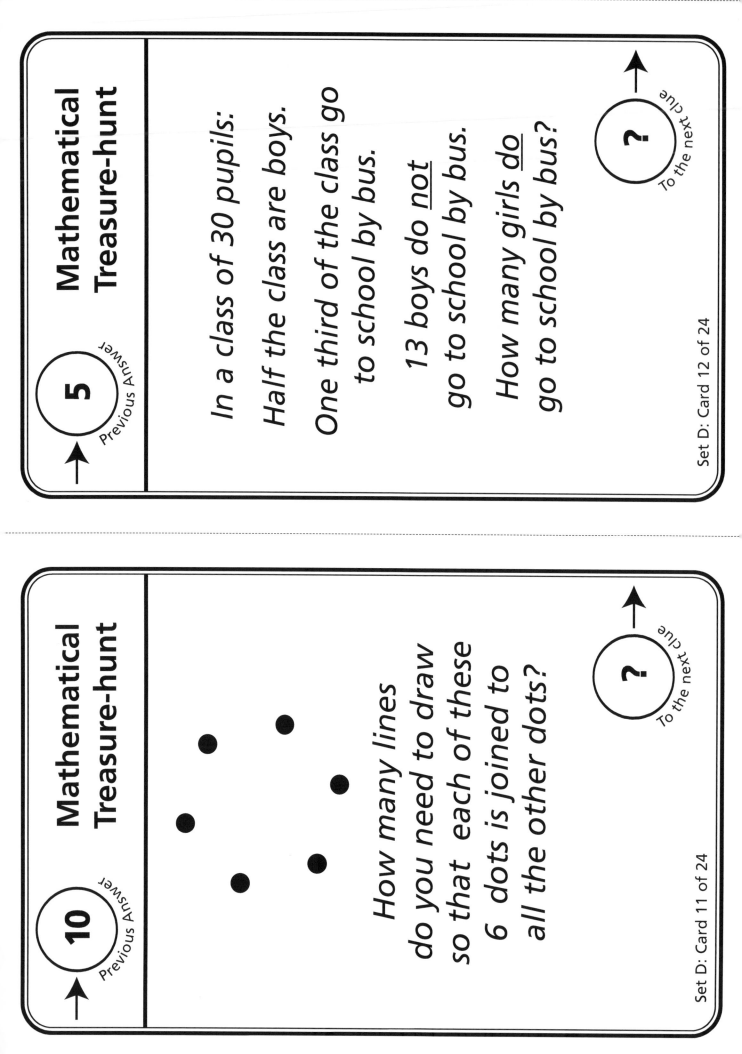

How many lines do you need to draw so that each of these 6 dots is joined to all the other dots?

?

To the next clue

Set D: Card 11 of 24

Mathematical Treasure-hunt

15
Previous Answer

A palindromic number is the same written backwards, e.g. 535.

How many palindromic numbers are there between 200 and 400?

?
To the next clue

Set D: Card 14 of 24

Mathematical Treasure-hunt

17
Previous Answer

In my purse I have five coins 1p, 2p, 5p, 10p, 20p.

How many different sums of money can I make with these coins?

Hint:
Check all possible totals from 1p to 38p.

?
To the next clue

Set D: Card 13 of 24

Mathematical Treasure-hunt

23 Previous Answer

A factor of a number is a number that will divide exactly into it.

E.g. the factors of 12 are 1, 2, 3, 4, 6 and 12.

How many factors has the number 48?

? To the next clue

Set D: Card 16 of 24

Mathematical Treasure-hunt

31 Previous Answer

Look at this bus timetable:

Bus Stop

Bus Station	10.45
The Library	10.49
Market Place	10.58
Church Street	11.04
City Hospital	11.15

How many minutes does it take to get from the Library to the City Hospital?

? To the next clue

Set D: Card 15 of 24

Mathematical Treasure-hunt

Previous Answer

34

8 people entered a knock-out competition of singles tennis (e.g. Round 1: 4 games, round 2: 2 games etc.)

If a new ball was used for each game, how many balls were needed altogether?

To the next clue

?

Set D: Card 18 of 24

Mathematical Treasure-hunt

Previous Answer

11

Susan & Mary were each given the same amount of money. Susan bought 4 peaches and had 4p left over.

Mary bought 3 peaches and had 13p left over.

How many pence did one peach cost?

To the next clue

?

Set D: Card 17 of 24

Mathematical Treasure-hunt

36
Previous Answer

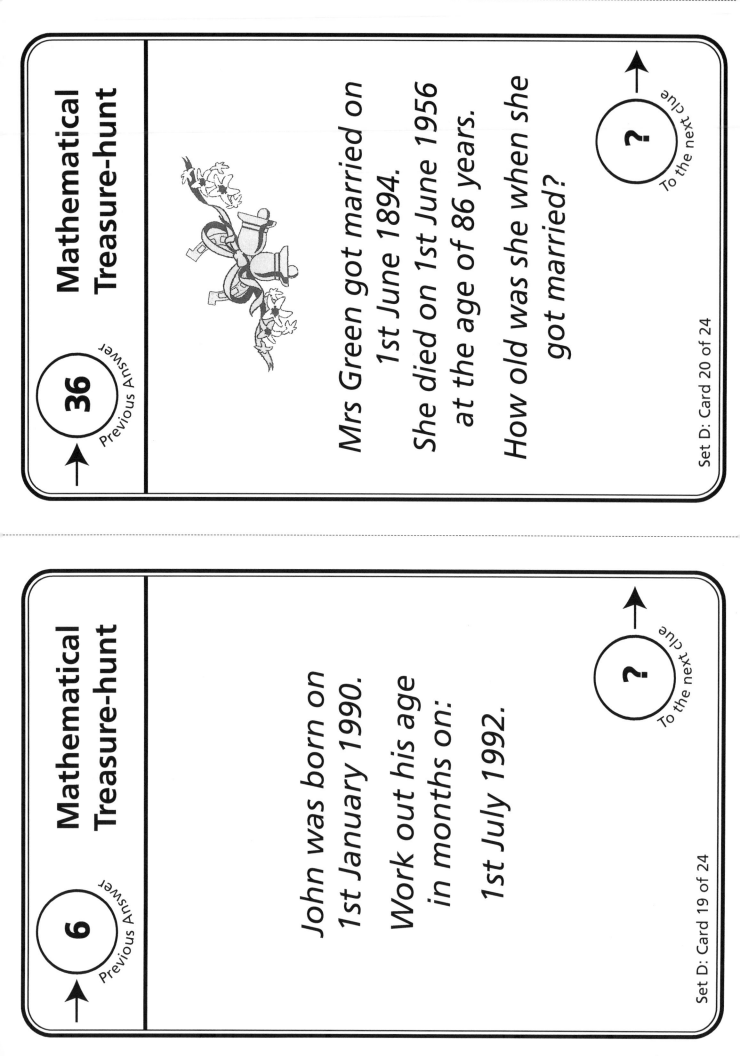

Mrs Green got married on 1st June 1894.

She died on 1st June 1956 at the age of 86 years.

How old was she when she got married?

?
To the next clue

Set D: Card 20 of 24

Mathematical Treasure-hunt

6
Previous Answer

John was born on 1st January 1990.

Work out his age in months on:

1st July 1992.

?
To the next clue

Set D: Card 19 of 24

Card 21

Mathematical Treasure-hunt

26
← Previous Answer

How many triangles are there in this diagram?

Hint:
They are not all the same size!

? To the next clue →

Set D: Card 21 of 24

Card 22

Mathematical Treasure-hunt

21
← Previous Answer

1, 3, 6, 10, ... etc are Triangular Numbers.

Work out the 8th triangular number.

1

1 + 2 = 3

1 + 2 + 3 = 3

1 + 2 + 3 + 4 = 10

? To the next clue →

Set D: Card 22 of 24

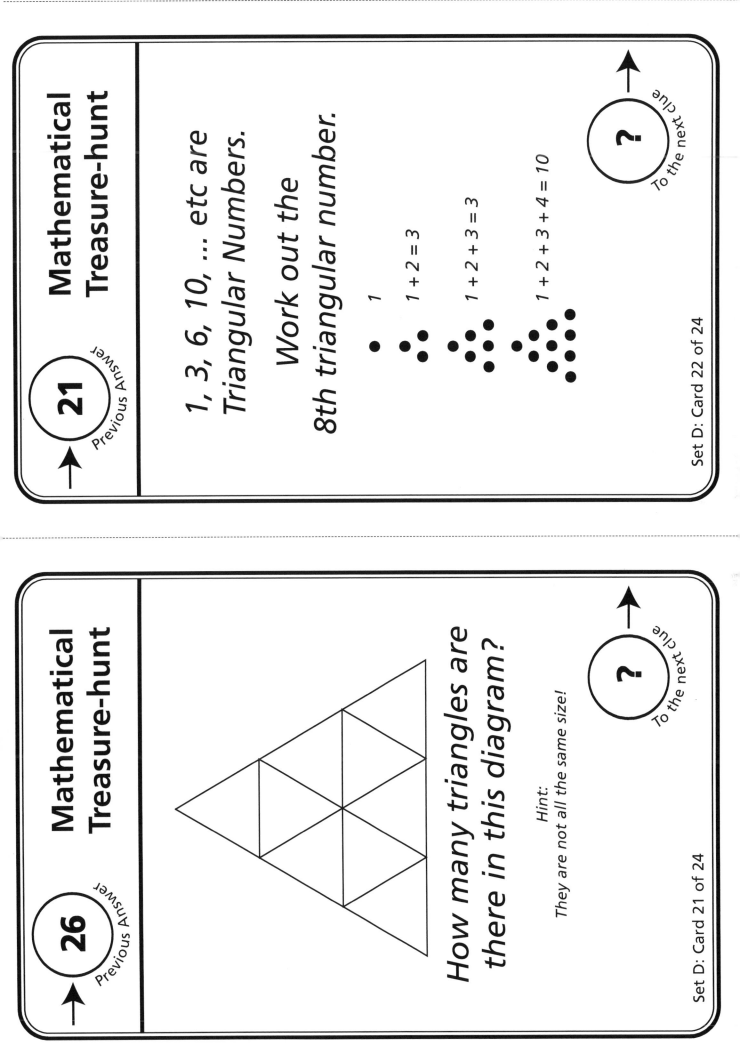

Mathematical Treasure-hunt

33

Previous Answer

In a darts game the score was 102 before Bill's turn.

His darts hit a 4, a double 20 and a treble 8.

What score remained after Bill's turn?

?

To the next clue

Set D: Card 24 of 24

Mathematical Treasure-hunt

13

Previous Answer

What is the total number of dominoes needed to make a set?

Hint:
Start at double blank and write down all pairs of numbers up to double six - be logical!

?

To the next clue

Set D: Card 23 of 24

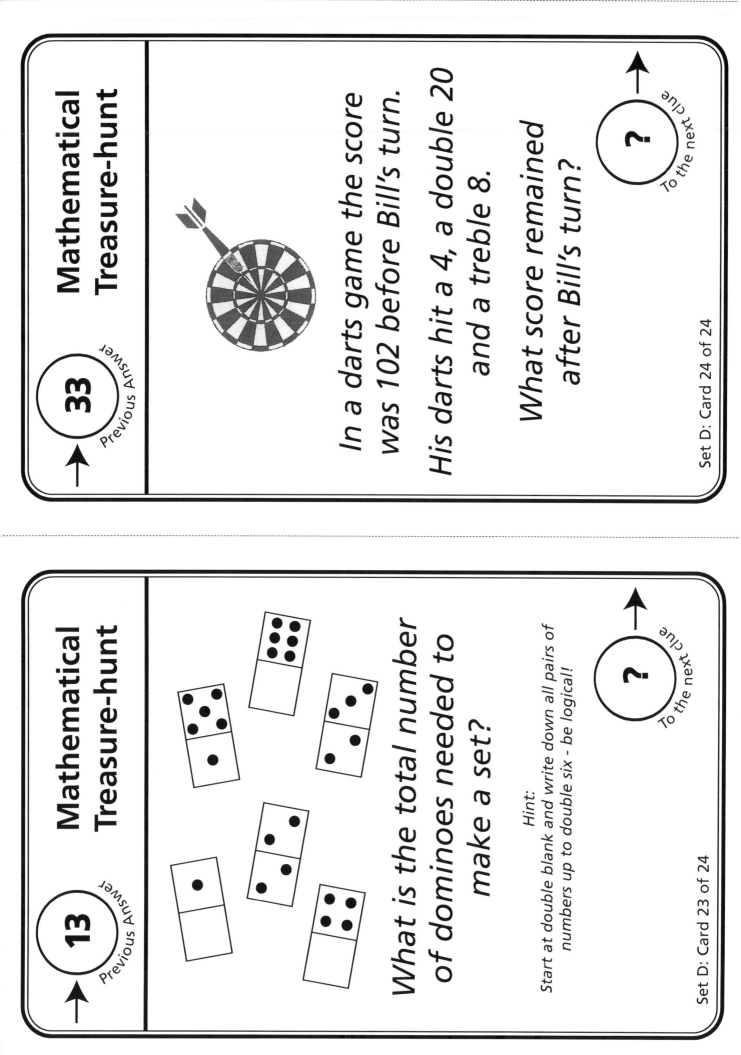

This is a good example of a complete treasure-hunt with 16 cards which covers a very wide range of topics and which will offer quite a challenge to some groups. The arrows show the sequence which the pattern of questions and answers follows. No reference numbers are given although it is helpful to add them to the full-size cards. It is best to distribute these reference numbers at random among the 16 cards in order to avoid them falling in sequence with the cyclic order of the answers.

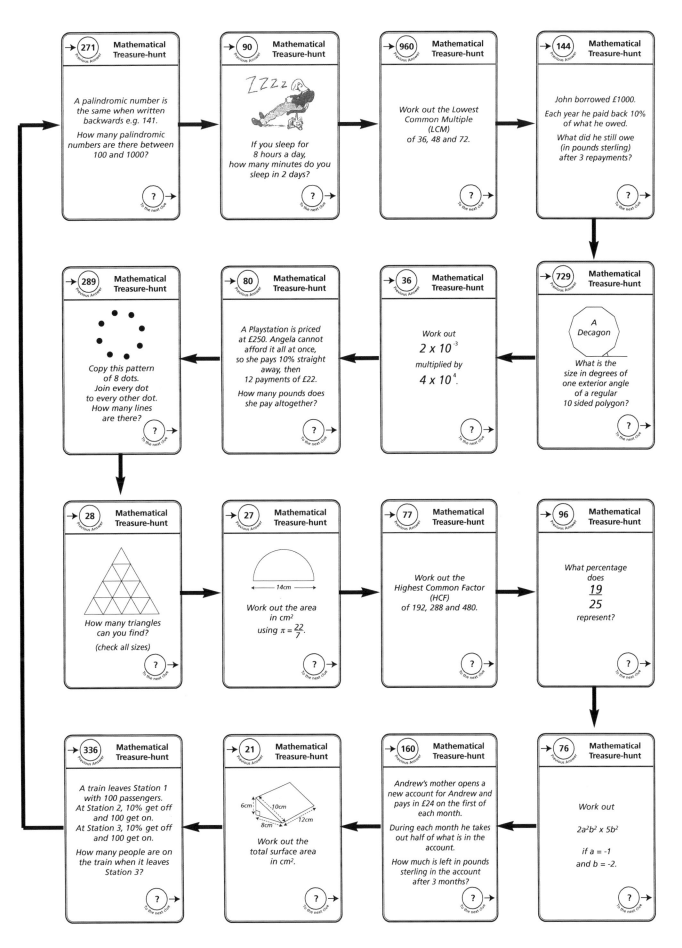

271 — Mathematical Treasure-hunt
Previous Answer

A palindromic number is the same when written backwards e.g. 141.

How many palindromic numbers are there between 100 and 1000?

? To the next clue

90 — Mathematical Treasure-hunt
Previous Answer

ZZZz

If you sleep for 8 hours a day, how many minutes do you sleep in 2 days?

? To the next clue

960 — Mathematical Treasure-hunt
Previous Answer

Work out the Lowest Common Multiple (LCM) of 36, 48 and 72.

? To the next clue

144 — Mathematical Treasure-hunt
Previous Answer

John borrowed £1000.

Each year he paid back 10% of what he owed.

What did he still owe (in pounds sterling) after 3 repayments?

? To the next clue

289 — Mathematical Treasure-hunt
Previous Answer

Copy this pattern of 8 dots. Join every dot to every other dot. How many lines are there?

? To the next clue

80 — Mathematical Treasure-hunt
Previous Answer

A Playstation is priced at £250. Angela cannot afford it all at once, so she pays 10% straight away, then 12 payments of £22.

How many pounds does she pay altogether?

? To the next clue

36 — Mathematical Treasure-hunt
Previous Answer

Work out

2×10^{-3}

multiplied by

4×10^{4}.

? To the next clue

729 — Mathematical Treasure-hunt
Previous Answer

A Decagon

What is the size in degrees of one exterior angle of a regular 10 sided polygon?

? To the next clue

28 — Mathematical Treasure-hunt
Previous Answer

How many triangles can you find?
(check all sizes)

? To the next clue

27 — Mathematical Treasure-hunt
Previous Answer

← 14cm →

Work out the area in cm² using $\pi = \frac{22}{7}$.

? To the next clue

77 — Mathematical Treasure-hunt
Previous Answer

Work out the Highest Common Factor (HCF) of 192, 288 and 480.

? To the next clue

96 — Mathematical Treasure-hunt
Previous Answer

What percentage does

$\frac{19}{25}$

represent?

? To the next clue

336 — Mathematical Treasure-hunt
Previous Answer

A train leaves Station 1 with 100 passengers. At Station 2, 10% get off and 100 get on. At Station 3, 10% get off and 100 get on.

How many people are on the train when it leaves Station 3?

? To the next clue

21 — Mathematical Treasure-hunt
Previous Answer

6cm — 10cm
8cm — 12cm

Work out the total surface area in cm².

? To the next clue

160 — Mathematical Treasure-hunt
Previous Answer

Andrew's mother opens a new account for Andrew and pays in £24 on the first of each month.

During each month he takes out half of what is in the account.

How much is left in pounds sterling in the account after 3 months?

? To the next clue

76 — Mathematical Treasure-hunt
Previous Answer

Work out

$2a^2b^2 \times 5b^2$

if $a = -1$ and $b = -2$.

? To the next clue

This is a good example of how a treasure-hunt can be tailored to deal with a very specific topic and be constructed for a particular group. In this case it deals with the circle theorems and it seems to take about fourteen cards to cover the topic thoroughly. It could be used to give impetus to a final revision, instead of a test. Large clear diagrams are essential.

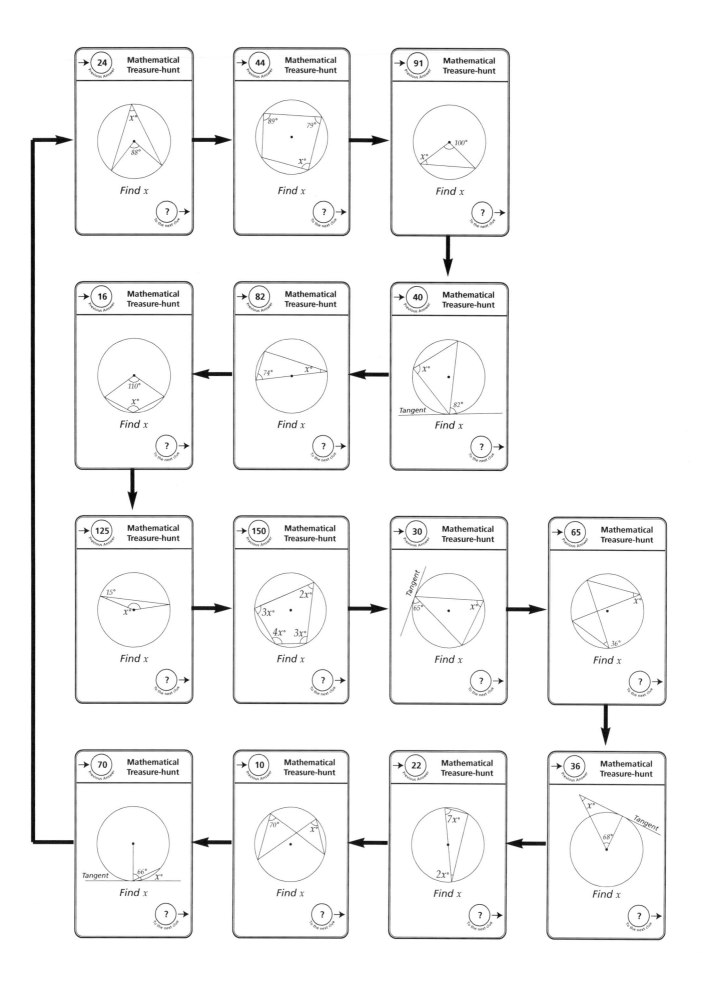

Extending the interest and the time taken

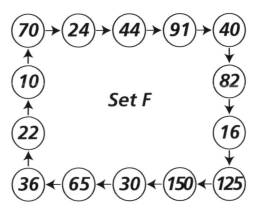

Set F

In the treasure-hunt opposite there are only 14 cards altogether and if the theorems are well understood, it would not take very long for the contestants to spot each value of x on each card and so move rapidly on to the next.

Indeed, they could compete the whole circuit so quickly that its value as an activity is very much reduced. Something extra is required to give more substance and body to the treasure-hunt.

91		C	Y	C	L	I	C	Q	U	A	D	R	I	L	A	T	E	R	A	L
40				I	S	O	S	C	E	L	E	S	T	R	I	A	N	G	L	E
24				R	A	D	I	U	S	A	N	D	T	A	N	G	E	N	T	
16	S	E	M	I	C	I	R	C	L	E										
44		A	N	G	L	E	A	T	C	E	N	T	R	E						
65		A	L	T	E	R	N	A	T	E	S	E	G	M	E	N	T			
125		A	N	G	L	E	A	T	C	E	N	T	R	E						
36	S	A	M	E	S	E	G	M	E	N	T									
150		I	S	O	S	C	E	L	E	S	T	R	I	A	N	G	L	E		
70		S	A	M	E	S	E	G	M	E	N	T								
10			S	E	M	I	C	I	R	C	L	E								
82		A	L	T	E	R	N	A	T	E	S	E	G	M	E	N	T			
22			R	A	D	I	U	S	A	N	D	T	A	N	G	E	N	T		
30			C	Y	C	L	I	C	Q	U	A	D	R	I	L	A	T	E	R	A	L

A useful possibility is to construct a type of crossword like this one which the teams have to fill in as they go round. At each card they have to enter an appropriate reason for the answer.

To give an extra dimension to the process, it can be constructed so that a further word or phrase reads downwards through the reasons. In this example the words which appear are are related to the topic being dealt with. However, the teacher could arrange the reasons in such an order that the linking word is something specific and appropriate to their school or class.

Some suggestions for further extension activities

With any treasure-hunt, not just geometrical ones, some teams may finish much sooner than others and it is always a good plan to have some extra activities or tasks ready to bring out if they are needed. The set of answers provides a ready made and appropriate set of useful numbers about which problems and questions can easily be fashioned. It might be helpful to call them 'bonus questions'.

Here are a few suggestions. No doubt others will immediately spring to mind, especially since in general the interests and abilities of the group will be known. Many of them of course depend on the particular set of answer numbers available and will need to be adapted to circumstances.

1. Find the sum of all the answers.
2. Add the five largest numbers from the answers and then subtract the five smallest.
3. Find the difference between the sum of all the odd numbers and the sum of all the even numbers.
4. Collect the answers into categories: primes, triangular numbers, perfect squares etc.
5. Counting the days from January 1st, what are the dates of the three largest answers?
6. Which answer is nearest to a multiple of 13 or 17 or whatever?
7. Find three or four answers that form an arithmetic progression.
8. Which two numbers multiplied together give a third number?
9. Write the three largest answers in binary form.
10. Add an extra digit to those answers which do not divide by 9 to create numbers which do.

And so on....

Answer Sheet

Team_____ **Time taken**_____

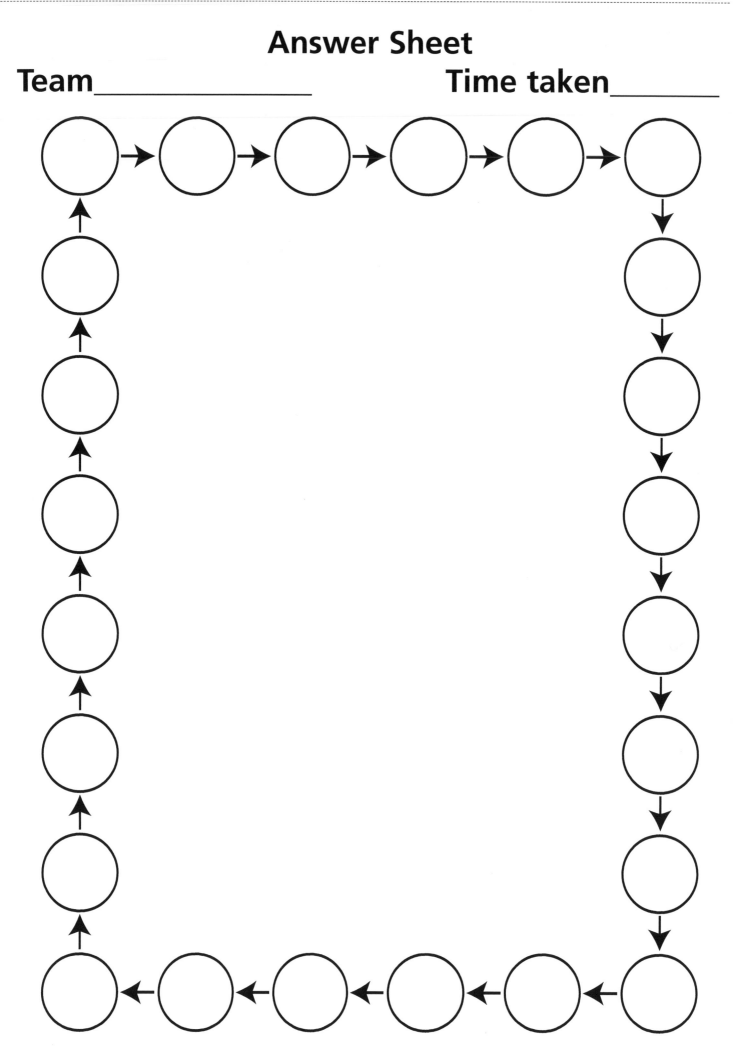